Get rid of
your gut

Get rid of
your gut

52 brilliant little ideas for a sensational six pack

Steve Shipside & Eve Cameron

brilliantideas

CAREFUL NOW

The tips in this book will help you enhance your abdominal area – if you follow them. But that's the important thing – you do have to put the ideas into practice; you can't expect us to do all the hard work for you. This book isn't a substitute for professional medical advice, so if you're thinking of making radical changes to your diet or exercise regime then you should consult your doctor. Washboard abs are within your reach, so go for it!

Infinite ideas would like to thank Steve Shipside, Eve Cameron, Dr Rob Hicks and Dr Ruth Chambers for their contributions to this book.

Copyright © The Infinite Ideas Company Limited, 2007

The right of the contributors to be identified as the author of this book has been asserted in accordance with the Copyright, Designs and Patents Act 1988.

First published in 2007 by
The Infinite Ideas Company Limited
36 St Giles
Oxford, OX1 3LD
United Kingdom
www.infideas.com

A CIP catalogue record for this book is available from the British Library
ISBN: 978-1-905940-22-6

Brand and product names are trademarks or registered trademarks of their respective owners.

Designed by Baseline Arts Ltd, Oxford
Typeset by Sparks, Oxford
Printed in China

Brilliant ideas

Rowing can be great for your core strength, but why do so many users look less like Steve Redgrave and more like Mr Bean?

Sociable, mood-enhancing, delicious ... but alcohol can also be ruinous to your waistline.

Weddings, birthdays, anniversaries, new job, new home – they are all great excuses for a party and could lead you into temptation.

Being groomed and stylish is important whether you're just starting out on your weight loss plan or already beginning to change shape.

What's in your lunch box today? Breakfast might be the most important meal of the day, but you shouldn't ignore lunch.

Swimming is one of the best all-round exercises, but most of us are no better than we were at school. Learn to cut a dash as you splash.

Slimming clubs promise results, but will they make more of a dent in your pocket than your fat reserves?

What has sleep got to do with weight loss? Get your pyjamas on. I'll tuck you in and explain.

Eating less and working out harder will result in weight loss. Simple.

It has a little healthy eating logo on it, so it must be good for you, right? No! Learn to read labels and help yourself lose weight.

Introduction

In your twenties you could consume pints of
lager and post-pub curries with abandon and
still look good in your skin-tight t-shirt the
next day. But the closer you get to forty, the
clearer it becomes that you can't go on treating
your body this way. Both our authors have been there and eaten that,
but more importantly managed to stop the middle-aged spread in its
tracks and, with a little effort, reclaimed the bodies they know they
deserve.

Eve's wake-up call occurred on her thirty-fifth birthday when she
suddenly caught sight of the spare-tyre hanging over the top of her
jeans. Holding her tummy in, walking taller and even a different
pair of jeans failed to sort out the problem, so she devised a host of
healthy-eating ideas which also helped her lose weight. Steve is an
IronMan triathlete, ultrarunner and marathoner. But before he was
superfit he wasn't, and it was only a trip to the doctor, who told him
he was well on his way to chronic back pain (through hauling his
burgeoning beer-belly around), that made him think about getting
himself into shape. The tips and tricks he picked up on his journey
from slob to athlete can help you shift your gut too.

You've probably tried diets before and may even have made a few trips to the gym or taken part in some excrcise classes. But quite quickly the deprivation and routine of a diet and exercise regime sends you scurrying for the biscuit tin. Eve and Steve are real people with real-world ideas for improving your physique. They know it's hard to find the time to visit the gym every day so have devised strategies for making the most of the time you can spend there as well as suggesting alternative forms of exercise you can incorporate into your everyday life. They know that deprivation is ultimately counter-productive so all their 'diet' suggestions are about eating intelligently rather than avoiding all foods that give you pleasure. Above all they know that a little know-how goes a long way so here they've supplied you with the information and tips you can use to build a gut-reduction plan that works for you. Here's to that sensational six-pack.

1. Stop the middle-aged spread!

As you get older, gaining weight is easier and losing weight is harder. Here are a couple of common reasons why.

There's no doubt that after the age of thirty it gets much harder to shake off excess weight. This is particularly annoying if you don't think you're overeating. There could be some good reasons why this is happening, as well as some good excuses.

Could you have a thyroid problem?
An underactive thyroid (hypothyroidism) is a common condition, especially in women, and its classic symptom is weight gain. The thyroid gland controls how quickly calories are burned up. When you have an underactive thyroid, your metabolism will be sluggish, you'll probably feel tired and low. If you suspect a thyroid problem, see your doctor.

Here's an idea for you...

Your environment can have a huge impact on how much you eat. The noisy, colourful atmosphere in fast food restaurants stimulates the appetite. Relax over your food in a more subdued atmosphere.

Defining idea …

'Several excuses are always less
convincing than one.'
ALDOUS HUXLEY

Is stress making you fat?

Some people barely eat anything when they're under pressure, but for most of us the opposite is true. Our bodies react by saying, 'We need extra fuel here to cope', and release the hormone cortisol, which helps us to use glucose stores for fuel. Cortisol stays in the bloodstream after the stress levels have calmed down, continuing to stimulate the appetite. So, stress makes your body want food, even though it hasn't actually burned off any extra calories.

Try two things. Make sure that you have a good supply of healthy snacks in anticipation of stressful moments. And in the longer term, you need to find ways of dealing with that stress through exercise, massage, therapy or maybe even a serious life change.

We can always make excuses for why we've put weight on. Think about the real reasons. Is your life sedentary? Do you eat enormous portions? Do you snack without even noticing? If you're always making excuses to yourself, you'll never reach your goals.

2. Does being overweight really matter?

OK, you're overweight. Perhaps you've lost your shape – or maybe you have always been a little on the plump side. Is it really a problem?

Many older people are incredibly proud of their size 10 frames, but look at least ten years older with their dried-up faces and flat little bottoms. A couple of extra kilos can be flattering, can't they? So when is a little plumpness unacceptable?

If carrying a *few* extra kilos doesn't bother you, it is not a health issue. If it diminishes your confidence, you should do something. If you have more than a few, it starts to matter and when you're properly overweight it matters very much indeed.

Here's an idea for you ...

If you are apple-shaped, with more fat around your middle, your risk of heart disease is greater than if you're pear-shaped, with more fat on your bottom. Divide your waist by your hip measurement. If the result is more than 0.95 for a man or 0.87 for a woman, you are apple-shaped.

15

Defining idea ...

'Imprisoned in every fat man a thin one is wildly signalling to be let out.'
CYRIL CONNOLLY

In the UK, an estimated two-thirds of men and half of women are over-weight. Experts are predicting that one in four adults will be obese – that is at least 12.5 kg (28 lb) overweight – by 2010.

Obesity makes everyday life uncomfortable. It's also the commonest cause of potentially fatal diseases. Even dental decay is more common in overweight people.

Here are some fat facts:

- 30% of deaths from coronary heart disease are directly linked to an unhealthy diet.
- A weight gain of just 10 kg doubles your risk of heart disease.
- Reducing your weight even by 5 kg can have a beneficial effect on cholesterol levels.
- A recent report suggested that as many as 40% of cancers have a dietary link.

There's still a lot of research to be done, but it is certain that being overweight isn't fun and it isn't clever – and it can be about a lot more than the way you look.

3. The fat of the land

Body fat is not all bad. Let's get a feel of why some body fat can be good.

Many think our bodies should be fat-free, but the fat under the skin and surrounding the body has many different functions. It's necessary for body protection; it insulates the organs and tissues; and it's involved in temperature regulation.

Some fat is vital, but too much indicates potential future illness. How much is too much? Try working out percentage body fat – the amount of fat tissue in your body as a percentage of total body weight.

Scales, callipers or a simple look in the mirror is often enough, but the most accurate methods involve high-tech equipment. Dual energy X-ray absorptiometry or DEXA uses a whole body scanner and two different low-dose X-rays to read bone and soft tissue mass, measuring fat percentage

Here's an idea for you ...

Work out your body fat percentage quickly by using a body fat scale or bioelectrical impedance analyser (look in pharmacists and gyms). Just don't test too often – every 4–8 weeks is best.

Defining idea ...

'It's simple: if it jiggles, it's fat.'
ARNOLD SCHWARZENEGGER

and where most of your fat is – as if this is something you don't already know. With hydrostatic weighing, or 'drowning on scales', you sit on a scale inside a tank of water, blow out as much air as you can, and are dunked under the water. Fat is lighter than water so the more you have the more you will float.

Skin fold thickness can be measured with calipers at your triceps, biceps, under the shoulder blade and just above the hip – you know, where you might try and 'pinch an inch'. The measurements are put into a formula to calculate your body fat. Not as accurate as DEXA or hydrostatic weighing, but more accessible.

Tracking your body fat is the best way to make sure that you're losing fat and gaining muscle.

If you're making an effort but your weight doesn't fall, you may have been losing fat but building muscle mass (which is heavier).

4. A weighty issue (or a weighty question)

If your waistband's been feeling a little tighter recently, here's how to work out roughly the right weight for you, plus some news you can use about body shape.

Here's a simple equation. *For weight to remain the same 'calories in' must equal 'calories out'.* Currently for many people the balance is towards too many in (food) and not enough out (exercise). You don't need to do equations to learn this. Just look around you. Go into a coffee shop and it's not just people's coats that are hanging over the side of the chair; their buttocks are too.

We all have a BMI, or body mass index to give it its full name. Doctors have been referring to it for years, and now insurance companies are asking for it.

Being overweight puts you at risk of many health problems. The BMI is just a figure that gives an indication

Here's an idea for you ...

Many experts are now saying that abdominal fat is the killer. The ideal waist measurement for men is less than 95 cm (37 inches) and less than 80 cm (32 inches) for women.

19

Defining idea ...

'I'm not overweight. I'm just nine
inches too short.'
SHELLEY WINTERS

of whether you are overweight or
not, and if so how much risk being
overweight is for your health. The
higher the BMI, the greater the risk of
health problems.

Working out your BMI is easy. All you have to do is weigh yourself and
record the result in kilograms. Then measure your height in metres.
Then do the following sum:

weight (kg) divided by (height (m) × height (m)) = BMI

Example: You weigh 70 kg and you are 1.6 metres tall

70 ÷ (1.6 × 1.6) =
70 ÷ 2.56 = 27.34
BMI = 27.34

Check your own result against the ranges below.

BMI for men	BMI for women	
Under 20	under 19	underweight
20–24.9	19–24.9	normal
25–29.9	25–29.9	overweight
30 plus	30 plus	obese

5. Spot reduction: the facts and the fiction

How much can you change your natural shape?

As well as your gender and your nutrition in childhood, the main influence on your body shape comes from your parents. You can take after one or other of them, or be a mix of both.

Broadly speaking, there are three main human body shapes.

- *Ectomorphs*: tall, thin and often quite angular, with low body fat percentage and not much muscle. Likely to put on weight around the stomach with age.
- *Mesomorphs*: quite a bit of muscle, a higher muscle-to-fat ratio than the other two. Stays in good shape if active, gains fat if sedentary.
- *Endomorphs*: rounder and softer looking, with more fat than mus-cle. Put weight on easily, but can achieve good muscle tone.

Here's an idea for you ...

To reduce your waistline, try exercising for ten minutes a day with a hula hoop – this can whittle inches from your waistline.

Defining idea …

'I'm in shape. Round is a shape, isn't it?'
ANONYMOUS

You can also have an android or gynoid influence. The android is an apple shape, with most weight carried on the top half of the body (and of course, sooner or later around the abdominal area). The gynoid influence, which is a pear shape, i.e. heavier on the bottom half, is a more female shape. Most of us do tend to fall into one type or the other.

Movers and shapers
We all tend to lose weight from the top down: face first, then chest and stomach, hips, thighs and legs. A fat pear-shaped person will slim into, well, a slimmer pear-shaped person. And there's not a lot more you can do about your basic shape apart from surgery, which I don't recommend, but it's up to you.

Exercise can increase your muscle bulk or streamline your muscles. However, if you've got lots of fat covering your muscles it will be harder to see muscle definition. You could just end up looking bigger. It's best to lose some body fat first.

6. Setting goals (without having to move the goalposts)

Creeping weight gain can catch you offside. Here's the smarter way to score your gut-busting goals.

A 1950s study of some US students found that only three per cent wrote a set of life goals. A follow-up twenty years later discovered that the goal-setters were worth more than the other 97% put together – and were healthier and happier too.

Goal-setting is just as relevant to weight loss, but simply saying 'I want to lose weight' won't get you very far. Why? Because goals need to be SMART.

Specific
Write down how much weight you want to lose. Is this for a special occasion? For health reasons? Think around

Here's an idea for you ...

Choose an easy goal and try to achieve it by the end of next week. The more goals you score, the more positive you will be about tackling the next one.

Defining idea …

the 'why' of your goal. Once it's clear, you'll be in control.

Measurable

How will you measure you weight loss? By weighing yourself regularly? By dropping a clothing size? How often? Do what works for you.

Attainable

If you're not 100% happy, revisit your goal to see if it is too ambitious. It does have to stretch you, but if it seems unattainable you'll soon become downhearted.

Realistic

If you are 165 cm (5 ft 5 in) and pear-shaped, no diet is going to turn you into Elle McPherson – especially if you're a man! Think in terms of being the best you can be.

Time-framed

Set a start point – 'I will start my weight loss plan on Thursday' – and an end – 'I will lose five kilos by the summer.'. Use positive language: there's no room here for 'might' and 'ought to'.

Your goal should be looking so clear that you can reach out and touch it. Game on!

7. Food accountancy made simple

You can eat them, count them or ignore them, but calories are the key to losing weight.

Calories are the basic units by which the energy values of food and the energy needs of the body are measured. Most foods are a combination of protein, fat and carbohydrate in different ratios. Gram for gram, fat contains 9 calories, protein and carbohydrates 4 calories and alcohol 7 calories. If you eat anything in excess, there's the potential that it will be more than your body needs and will end up stored as fat.

How many calories do you need?
Here's a basic formula. Other factors come in – your age, your sex – but this gives you a steer.

1   Work out your *resting metabolic rate* (RMR). Multiply your weight in pounds by 10 if you're a woman, or 11 if you're a man.

Here's an idea for you …

Eat soya products. A particular isoflavone in soya may hold the key to improving the rate at which your cells burn up fat. It boosts your metabolism and reduces your appetite.

Defining idea ...

2 Factor in how active you are by multiplying the sum above by: 0.2 if you only do light activities, 0.3 if you do a formal exercise such as walking, 0.4 if you are moderately active or 0.5 if you do manual labour or lots of sports. This is the number of calories you need on top of your RMR.

3 Eating and digesting food uses up around 10% of your calorie needs, so, after adding your RMR and the extra calories for your activity level, work out 10%.

4 Add all three of those figures together for your total calorie needs per day.

To lose a pound a week, you need to cut your daily calories by 500 (or lose them through exercise). OK, end of accountancy lesson. Who'd have thought numbers could be such fun?

8. Come on, it's time for breakfast

If you miss breakfast you're missing out big-time.

Overnight the body undergoes a mini-fast, so no matter who or where you are, your natural instinct is to eat soon after you get up. Eating breakfast not only fulfils this need and is an excellent way to start the day, but getting some proper food into you first thing will lessen the chance of you suffering unhealthy snack attacks later. Yes, that cake, biscuit or chocolate bar sure does taste good, but it provides too much sugar, too quickly. Before long you'll be reaching for another, and another, and another …

If you don't usually have breakfast, try it. A glass of orange juice, some fruit, a couple of slices of toast are just some of the simple ways to give you a heads-up. They'll give you energy that's released gradually, so that you don't start to flag early on. You'll feel better, you'll have more energy and

Here's an idea for you …

Fill the kettle for your first cuppa of the day. Flick the switch. Now, while the kettle is boiling, eat a bowl of cereal. Enjoy it. You have time.

Defining idea ...

'It is well to be up before daybreak, for such habits contribute to health, wealth, and wisdom.'
ARISTOTLE

you'll not be eating so many unhealthy snacks. If you only have a banana and a glass of fruit juice, then you've also had two of your target five portions of fruit and vegetables for the day.

You could eat something on your way to work. A few dried apricots, a banana or a yoghurt drink are easy to have on the go. You could have breakfast at work (cereal box in the desk drawer, sorted). But be honest, will spending ten minutes to have breakfast before you start work make that much difference? In fact, it will mean you are more productive during the rest of the morning. You'll probably end up saving that time and more.

More importantly, eating breakfast means you won't get those hunger pangs before your day's work has even begun.

9. Off the bus, up the stairs

Did you know it's possible to exercise during the working day without even thinking about it?

We're working longer, with greater workloads, to tighter deadlines than ever. So when experts recommend doing 30 minutes of moderately intense physical activity five days a week, at first glance the equation doesn't seem to work. But there are solutions.

First, the 30 minutes doesn't have to be all in one go. It can be 15-minute, 10-minute or even 5-minute blocks. And it doesn't need to be exercise as such. Getting up to see a colleague rather than sending an email, going to a local coffee shop rather than the staff kitchen, these all count. You don't need to be sweating; you just need to feel warm and slightly out of breath.

Here's an idea for you ...

Make a virtue out of a necessity. Use a loo on a different floor than usual, or further away. Or try going to the bathroom every two hours, whether you feel the need or not.

Defining idea …

'A man's health can be judged by which he takes two at a time – pills or stairs.'
JOAN WELSH

Look at your daily routine
Think how you can be more active, at each stage of your day. Here are some ideas.

- Instead of having your morning newspaper delivered, walk to the newsagent and buy it.
- Walk with your children to school.
- Walk or cycle to work – or get off the bus one stop earlier and walk the rest of the way.
- Use the stairs rather than the lift, or take a slightly longer route to your work area.
- Go up and down the stairs twice each time – you'll soon feel your heart rate increasing.
- Walk to and from your desk while waiting for the photocopier.
- Try taking a slightly longer route to the copier, and walk briskly.
- If you are having a meeting, don't find a room – try walking while you are talking instead.

Amazing, isn't it? By lunchtime, you could have already done your 30 minutes.

10. Pump that body

The thought of Lycra-clad rippling bodies may send you reaching for the donuts. But the gym offers so much more. Come and have a look.

You either love the gym or you loathe it. So what's the appeal? Well, to start with, just visiting the gym is an outing and offers the chance to meet people. You can ogle the beautiful ones (discreetly), including yourself in the mirror without being labelled a poser. You can watch wall-to-wall TV too. And, of course, you can exercise (easily forgotten, but true).

If you walk or cycle to the gym, you'll have probably done enough exercise without even going in – but if you do, there's a variety box on offer. Aerobics, circuits, free and fixed resistance machine weights, rowers, bikes, balls ... something to suit everyone, for strength, cardiovascular fitness, flexibility, body shape, and of course weight.

Here's an idea for you ...

Ask your gym for a free trial session. At the least, you'll get a bit of attention and be able to see what it's like. At best, you may just discover your new home.

33

Defining idea ...

'Training gives us an outlet for
suppressed energies created by stress
and thus tones the spirit just as
exercise conditions the body.'
ARNOLD SCHWARZENEGGER

If you get out of breath exercising,
you are cardio-training: your heart
and lungs will be working harder and
your fitness will be improving. While
exercising you should be burning fat
too, which is, after all, what you want.

Get in the zone

To burn fat efficiently, you need to be in your optimum training zone.
No, this isn't the part of the gym where you feel happiest. It's the
heart rate you need to be working at if you want to lose weight.

Your optimum training zone is between 70–90% of your maximum
heart rate (MHR). To find it subtract your age in years from 220 to get
your MHR, then multiply your MHR by, let's say, 0.8 (80%). This is the
maximum number of heartbeats per minute you should have during
your workout to efficiently burn fat.

11. Shape up from home

You don't have to join an expensive gym to lose weight and get fit. Try staying in.

Exercising from home fits in with almost any lifestyle and can work for every budget. Here are some ideas to help you burn fat in the comfort of your own castle.

Fitness videos
These are very cost effective, provided you don't simply file them beside your complete collection of Bond movies. Go for a variety so that you don't get bored, making sure that at least one has a body sculpting or resistance training section (use a resistance band or dumbbells for this – or a can of beans in each hand!) Do the resistance training section two or three times a week and the more aerobic section three to five times a week.

Here's an idea for you ...

If you've been running for a while, why not join a running club or sign up for a charity fun run? Check out www.coolrunning.com.

Defining idea ...

A home circuit

All you need are a skipping rope, a mat, some stairs and a resistance band. Warm up by walking up and down the stairs, then skip or stair-step for one minute, followed by twenty repetitions of a toning exercise with the resistance band (it comes with an exercise sheet). Do your minute's aerobic exercise again, followed by another toning session – stomach exercises this time. Continue the circuit for about fifteen minutes and aim to do it twice a week.

Running

This is a fantastic way to burn fat, tone your legs and boost your fitness. Running requires a good pair of running shoes and comfy clothing; do go to a specialist sports shop to get them. An easy way to start is to walk for a few minutes, then run for a few minutes, then walk again and so on. As you progress, you'll be running more and walking less!

12. Piling on the Pilates

The ballerinas' secret is now recognised as having benefits for everyone from recovering rugby players to recovering couch potatoes.

Joseph H. Pilates was no ballerina. A puny youth who suffered from rickets, asthma and rheumatic fever, he developed his now-famous technique to overcome his own physical weaknesses. He didn't have a modern gym to hand either; only time, a confined space and minimal equipment. Despite, or perhaps because of that, our Joseph forged himself a new body, and in the process a career as gymnast, boxer, circus performer and eventually physical educator.

The keys to Pilates are concentration, precise control of movement, an understanding of breathing, and building a strong physical core. And it's perfect for anyone looking to lose a spare tyre or two.

Here's an idea for you ...

Doing Pilates on a Swiss ball gives you the opportunity to stretch further than before while still being comfortably supported. It's also oddly soothing. Give it a go.

Defining idea …

'*Physical fitness is the first requisite of happiness.*'
JOSEPH H. PILATES

What can I expect?
You'll start with mat work. Initially a lot of work will focus on making you aware of specific parts of your body, in particular the muscles of your stomach. Next come simple movements such as rolling up into a sitting position: these help you realise how different parts of the body work together. The moves are done slowly, with emphasis on breathing correctly, and repetitions are few.

Sounds cushy? The concentration, plus the effort of tensing muscles in unfamiliar ways, makes for surprisingly hard work – but injuries are rare. Pilates suits all ages and levels of strength and flexibility, and promotes a general feeling of well-being.

Core blimey
Among the benefits of Pilates are a greater attention to the deeper lying muscles of the core, such as the transversus, which lies under the abs. For athletes, this core strength approach gives greater balance and power. Dancers appreciate the suppleness encouraged by moves, and there are those who swear that it improves posture so much that you can end up taller!

13. Eat, drink and be sweaty

If you're exercising to lose weight, you may need to eat and drink *more* ...

Eating and drinking may have led you to the gym, but now is not the time to stop. If you're trying to starve yourself and sweat your little cotton socks off at the same time, you're on a highway to grumpiness and burn out. If you want to get the most out of the gym, learn to snack for success.

Before
If you head for the gym first thing, have a light carb-based breakfast (like cereal). Breakfast bars can provide a good balance but many are high-fat and high-calorie. Snack on them all day and you might as well have eaten all the pies.

Here's an idea for you ...

Drinking fountains won't help you keep an eye on how much you drink. Take a large (three-quarters of a litre or more) drinking bottle with you and keep it to hand whenever you're in a class or on a machine.

Defining idea …

'Never eat more than you can lift.'
MISS PIGGY

- Protein. Yes, it's the building block for making muscle but it's a pig to digest.

Big no-nos before working out include:

- Sugary snacks. A short, sharp, sugar high followed later by a sugar low? You'll leave the gym feeling blue.

During
Drink! In an hour's intense exercise you can lose two pounds – but they're all water. If you don't put this back, your cells malfunction and your blood volume decreases. To rehydrate fast, opt 'isotonic' sports drinks: they are absorbed much faster than water because they more closely match the mineral balance of our body fluids.

After
Shoving food into your face immediately after exercise may seem to miss the point but it's important. First, you want to avoid an energy trough (it's so demotivating). Second, if you make huge energy demands on your body then don't feed it, you may be sending it the wrong messages. Reassure it by guzzling a sports bar, a sports drink or a banana.

14. How to be a smart (slim) shopper

You can save yourself pounds – both £££s and lbs – just by shopping wisely.

Losing weight means being a savvy shopper. What's the point of deciding you'll prepare a delicious low-fat meal if all you have in the house is pastry, sausages and some double cream? Haphazard shopping will cost you dear in the weight-loss stakes. Here are some things to think about:

- Do not go shopping when you're hungry. You'll be seduced by all the possibilities on offer. Have a meal or snack before you go.
- Take a list. You'll buy everything you really need and minimise the threat of impulse buys.
- Plan some easy, healthy meals you can cook yourself and shop for the fresh ingredients.
- Even if foods have a healthy eating or reduced fat logo, check the labels to see what you're really getting.

Here's an idea for you …

Chop bananas into bite-sized chunks and freeze them for healthy, delicious, almost ice-creamy treats to snack on. You can freeze grapes too.

41

Defining idea ...

'I can spend hours in a grocery store. I get so excited when I see food, I go crazy.'
CAMERON DIAZ

■ Avoid special offers, super-sizes and multi-buys unless they're healthy and low fat.

Apart from that, you just have to accept that supermarkets are run by clever people who want to sell you lots of things. If you can stay strong, your trolley should end up looking something like this:

In the trolley

■ Wholegrains
■ Low-fat dairy produce
■ Dried fruit to snack on
  – keep servings small
■ Low-fat/reduced-calorie cereal

■ Fruit and vegetables
■ Lean cuts of meat
■ Fish, including a portion or two of oily fish
■ Snack bars – but check the label

On the shelf

■ Cereals with added sugar
■ Sausages, meat pies and pasties
■ Battered and bread-crumbed meat and seafood

■ Biscuits and cakes, crisps
■ Anything with pastry
■ Jams and spreads (choose sugar-free versions)
■ Full fat ice-cream – why not try frozen yoghurt instead?

15. Balls

Ever wondered what those oversized beach ball things are for? They are waiting to tighten your tummy.

It's time to play ball. Swiss ball, that is. Swiss balls are soft and supportive, which means you can trust yourself to one and stretch in comfort. Being balls, however, everything you do perched on one, even sitting, involves a bit of balancing, working the muscles that control your core stability – and that translates to a flat stomach.

These balls come in different sizes, for different sized people. The key is being able to sit comfortably on top with your knees bent and feet flat on the floor. Roughly speaking a 45 cm diameter ball is for people 1.40–1.52 m tall (4 feet 7 inches–5 feet in old money); 55 cm balls for middle-sizers; and 65 cm balls for those 1.70–1.80 m tall (5 feet 7 inches to 5 feet 11 inches).

Note: These balls can take a full-grown man and a pair of dumbbells. And they don't explode – just deflate pathetically – so don't be afraid to bounce on them.

Defining idea …

*'Happiness is a ball after which we run
wherever it rolls, and we push it with
our feet when it stops.'*
JOHANN WOLFGANG VON GOETHE

Exercises to try

■ *Back stretch.*
Sit on the centre of the ball, with
feet a little way apart. Gently walk
your feet away so that you lie back
and both your back and neck are
supported on the ball. Now open your arms on each side and feel
the stretch across your back. Then stretch your arms over your
head and down as if reaching for the floor behind.

■ *Forward roll out.*
Kneel on the floor in front of your ball and lean forward slightly to
rest your forearms on the ball with hands together. Keeping your
abs good 'n' tight, gently roll the ball forward until your arms are
straight. Hold for a moment, then roll back to the start position.
Repeat.

16. Get the write habit

Noting down what you are eating may give you some surprises – and help you lose weight.

Keeping a diary is an invaluable tool, as it gives you a real insight into the kinds of foods you usually eat and the quantity and frequency of meals and snacks. Unless you know where you're going wrong, how can you put things right?

Try it for a week. At the end, study your diary and ask yourself the following questions:

■ Am I eating regularly (breakfast, lunch and dinner)?
  Skip a meal and you'll probably compensate by over-eating at the next one or indulging in high-calorie, fat-laden snacks.

■ How often am I eating between meals and what am I grazing on?
  If those in-between snacks are fruit or low-fat yoghurt, fine, but if

Here's an idea for you ...

For a few minutes every day, picture how you'll look when you've achieved your goal. It works for Olympic gold medal winners!

45

Defining idea ...

they are crisps, chocolate or an entire packet of biscuits (hey, we've all done it), that means weight gain.

■ Is my diet sufficiently varied? Am I eating the same foods day in, day out?

For optimum health we need proteins (meat, fish, eggs, pulses), carbohydrates (bread, cereal, pasta, rice, potatoes) and fruit and vegetables, plus some fats and dairy. How's your mix?

■ Do I rely on junk food and ready-prepared meals?

If you eat this way all the time, weight gain is inevitable. Serve side dishes of vegetables or salad, or better still, cook from scratch and impress yourself.

■ What am I drinking?

Alcohol is just empty calories – all pain, and no gain (except weight, of course) – and while some fizzy drinks contain up to seven teaspoons of sugar, fruit juice contains lots of natural sugar too. And are you drinking enough water?

Now make a list of what you can change. Start with the simplest changes and implement them quickly so you'll feel encouraged.

17. Roman revenge

You want a Stallone Six-Pack but that rock-hard belly is stubbornly refusing to show. How do you make that difference?

Are you burning away that fat only to find that the muscles underneath are more washout than washboard? Time for the torture apparatus.

Roman what?
Roman chairs come in a variety of shapes but they all look distinctly uncomfortable and have two basic features: a padded bar to tuck your lower legs under, and a larger pad to take the weight of your lower body (bum or groin, depending which way up you're facing).

Now what do I do?
The point of the Roman chair is that it makes your muscles work through a wider range of movement than usual – hyperextend – and if you have a weak back this could be dangerous. If in doubt, take professional advice.

Here's an idea for you ...

If you want more Roman torture, flip the other way up, lock your feet under the bar with your bum on the pad, and crunch. This way you have to keep tense all the time with no respite.

47

Defining idea ...

Make sure you're nicely warmed up then lie face down, with the backs of your calves tucked under the padded bar, your elbows bent and your hands on your ears. Smoothly bend forwards and extend your shoulders down. Bring your body back to horizontal, then arch upwards so you are lifting your shoulders and chest high off the horizontal. This will work your back muscles but you also have to tense your stomach muscles (and your buttocks) to maintain the position. That's a rep. Try ten to twelve more.

For killer obliques turn sideways on the chair and extend down and up. Don't attempt the same range of movement as you would face down as you won't make it and it will be very intense.

18. Don't try too hard

Simple food swaps, cutting back on treats and pushing yourself to be more active can help you achieve long-term weight loss.

Lose a little bit of weight every week with changes that are so simple, you'll barely notice them. It's possible to lose half a kilo (a pound) a week if you shave 500 calories per day from your food intake (or expend it through activity). Get started with the following clever little ideas:

Say no to crisps
A regular 40 g bag has around 200 calories and 10 g of fat. Even lighter versions come in at slightly over half of that amount. Stop having a bag each day = save at least 500 calories a week.

Avoid large portions
A large burger, fries and drink will easily stack up to 1000 calories. Opt for the regular or small sizes = save 500 calories.

Here's an idea for you ...

Chew sugar-free gum or after a meal or a snack. As well as cleaning your teeth, it sends a psychological message that you have finished eating and that it is time to do something else.

Defining idea ...

On your bike

Eco-friendly, fun and jolly good exercise. An hour's cycling = nearly 500 calories.

Sandwich swap

Have low-fat salad cream in your lunchtime sandwich instead of butter = save up to 500 calories a week.

Rethink your Saturday night take-away

Choose chicken chow mein and boiled rice over sweet and sour chicken and fried rice = save around 500 calories.

Walk more

Walk to work, the shops or just for fun (briskly, mind) = around 250 calories an hour.

Have a skinnier coffee

Opt for a semi-skimmed coffee rather than a full-fat cappuccino = save 170 calories.

Party snacks

Two tablespoons of taramasalata = 130 calories (tzatziki = around 40 calories). Thick meat pate on French bread = about 250 calories (smoked salmon on rye bread = 130 calories). A cocktail sausage = 70 calories (sausage roll = 200 calories).

19. Stairway to heaven

Shhh. The stepper's not just for buns of steel. You can get a full core-strength workout at the same time. Just don't tell anyone else ...

The humble stepper is possibly the most underused piece of kit in the whole gym, and all because of a simple misunderstanding. Most people see it as a means of toning the buttocks, and for some reason that means that it is largely left to the women. But the stepper can be your stairway to abs heaven. Here's how.

Get on the stepper, give it some – and let go
That's all there is to it. You see people resting their body weight on their arms (bad for the wrists), or hanging off backwards. What you don't see are people who let go and use their arms as counterbalances to their pumping legs. Let go, and now your legs are taking all your body weight, which

Here's an idea for you ...

With the resistance fairly low, try pumping the steps faster. Imagine the Tour de France riders are competing on unicycles and you are sprinting against Lance Armstrong for the *maillot jaune*. Now watch those calories burn off.

51

Defining idea …

'The journey of a thousand miles
starts with a single step.'
MAO TSE TUNG

massively increases the strength and
cardio benefits. Letting go forces you
to balance, which brings in all the
muscles of the torso – your obliques,
abs and back – and builds up core
strength. No matter how quickly or slowly you go, you will burn
calories at around twice the rate you get on a stationary bike and not
so much less than when you're on the treadmill. Unlike the treadmill,
however, the stepper remains a very low-impact activity with
minimal shock on the joints.

It's breathtakingly simple, very little known and changes absolutely
everything.

Others will queue for hours to get on the treadmill, while the step-
pers lie idle. Let them. Because the fewer people who understand the
potential of the stepper, the more machines there are for the rest of
us.

20. The birds and the bees

There's a lot to be said for putting some loving into slimming. Everyone does it, you know. Let's talk about sexercise.

Although you might be thinking you'd prefer a family-sized bar of fruit and nut, it's time to start thinking of sex as a powerful weapon in your weight-loss armoury.

Lesson 1

Sex is a great esteem-booster. You might feel self-conscious, but virtually all research shows that men have no idea what cellulite is and women go for personality, not looks (well, looks second). Don't dwell on what you don't like about your body; enjoy every compliment, even if it is only about your ears. You're just out of the shower, wrapped in a clean white towel, your hair damp, your body oiled, a hint of parfum … gosh, I'm getting quite carried away.

Here's an idea for you …

Try a sensual aromatherapy massage to get you both in a loving mood. Just add five drops of lavender, rose or chamomile oil to 20 ml of a carrier oil, such as almond or sunflower.

Defining idea …

'I'd like to meet the man who invented sex and see what he's working on now.'
ANONYMOUS

Lesson 2

Sex helps you win the battle of the bulge. According to a US study, making love three times week burns approximately 7,500 calories a year – the same as jogging 120 km (75 miles). Of course you do have to actively participate, as opposed to lying there wondering what you're going to eat tomorrow, but even kissing burns a few calories a minute.

Lesson 3

Sex helps you to sleep, which is a good thing (as long as it's not in the middle of a love session). Lack of sleep increases snacking and the urge for high-calorie, quick-energy foods.

Lesson 4

Sex makes you look younger and helps you stay healthy. It boosts your immune system and could help to reduce cholesterol levels. And of course, sex is a way of strengthening your relationship, which boosts your self-esteem, which means that anything is possible, including losing weight.

21. You're in good company

Being a groupie is not just about hanging around after celebrities ...

Why struggle on your own? Get hold of a few friends and make up your own group, or find one you can join. Then there'll be others to keep you on the straight and narrow, whatever you decide to do, who you'll have to face up to if you start cheating on your healthy resolve. They can give you a bit of competition, maybe to see who can lose the most weight or run the furthest or fastest – and can also keep up your interest in what you're doing.

You can get some of the same effects with just one other person. Keep up with a particular buddy who's getting healthy with you, or someone who's interested in your wellbeing. Telephone, text and email each other to chat through temptations and progress, and draw on each other's experience. Don't be shy about asking for their help. You can motivate each

Here's an idea for you ...

Book a club holiday where you'll have guaranteed company on any number of outdoor activities. Trying out a new sport or activity could give you a taste for it, so that you seek out a local club when you're back home again too.

Defining idea ...

other and keep reinforcing what you've got to gain by tackling your (mutual) weaknesses. Go and see them for a chat to stop yourself raiding the fridge or popping out to buy bottles of drink or boxes of chocolate.

You could even find a benefactor who'll bribe you to be good! A parent, maybe, even your partner? Agree what it is you're to achieve – and what the reward will be. Keep visualising the rewards and what you stand to lose if you don't make your goal. If you're a selfless person, motivated by helping others, then there's no reason why your reward can't be something to benefit other people rather than yourself.

22. Planks a lot

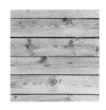

A way to a strong mid-section without moving at all? Time to get static.

Welcome to the wonderful world of isometrics: tensing a muscle without moving anything – either just by contracting it, or by applying a force to something that simply can't go anywhere. Stand in a doorway and try to push the frame apart Samson style. Nothing is moving (hopefully) but, my, can you feel the squeeze. So too with walking the plank. Here the whole point is to hold the body perfectly still. Because it's only supported on the ground at a couple of points, this requires quite a lot of muscular effort. Unlike crunches, which mainly work the rectus abdominis, the effort of keeping the stomach straight (and off the ground) requires the work of all the muscles including the obliques and the transversus abdominis. Which makes for a strong midsection.

Here's an idea for you ...

When you do the side plank, put a bit of a stretch down the other side of the body by sticking your 'spare' arm straight out sideways so it points at the ceiling, then over your head and hold.

Defining idea ...

'Mastering others is strength.
Mastering yourself is true power.'
Lao Tzu

The plank

Lie face down on a mat then lift up so you are resting your weight on your forearms and your toes (or your knees if toes proves too hard). Now hold that position absolutely rigidly. Your back should be straight – if your bum is sticking up, pull it back into line. If your hips or belly are sagging, then whip them back into line too. Keep going for as long as you can – time yourself and see if you can get any better.

The side plank

Start on your side and raise yourself onto your elbow with your body dead straight so that there is a long wedge of daylight underneath you from your elbow (which should be directly under your shoulder) down to your feet. This puts more of the stress on the obliques. When you can't hold it anymore roll over to your other side and repeat the process.

23. I'll have a 21, 34 and 52 please … oh and a large portion of 15

The road to Fatville is paved with takeaways, but you don't need to cut them out completely.

Eating takeaways is the norm for many of us. The trouble is you have no idea what you're really consuming in terms of fat and calories. Here are some tips on how to make less fattening choices.

Fish and chips
High in protein, some vitamins, plus a few minerals – but high in fat, low in fibre.

- Balance with a vitamin-packed salad and some low-fat protein, such as cottage cheese.
- Make your own. Stick a piece of fish under the grill and use low-fat oven chips.

Here's an idea for you …

Choose soup as a starter. It fills you up so there's less room for garlic bread or 'Death by Chocolate'.

59

Defining idea …

*'The journey of a thousand pounds
begins with a single burger.'*
CHRIS O'BRIEN

Pizza
Cheese and tomato offers protein,
calcium and some vitamins – but
pepperoni piles on fat.

■ Balance with a chicken casserole
   and vegetables for low-fat protein
   and plenty of fibre.

■ Make your own. Use a ready-made base. Top it with heaps of
   vegetables, a little protein (lean beef, tuna or grated cheese).

Beefburger, fries and a milkshake
High in protein and calcium, plus some vitamins – but high in
saturated fat, low in fibre.

■ Balance with a meal of wholemeal pasta and vegetables for fibre
   without the fat.

■ Make your own. Shape a burger from lean mince. Serve with
   potato wedges or use half a wholemeal roll. Make a milkshake
   with skimmed milk and flavoured powder.

When you order a take-away, follow these fat-reducing tips – and stop
eating when you are full!

■ Avoid anything fried: choose grilled, steamed, or baked.

■ Say no to creamy and buttery sauces.

■ Watch out for coconut – it's full of saturated fat.

■ Make your side order of rice plain boiled.

■ Leave out the garlic bread.

24. With friends like you, who needs enemies?

Having a poor body image is a surefire way to sabotage your diet, so shape up with a little self-love.

No one is immune from disliking their shape and looks, but some people seem to manage to get over the problem more readily. This is not easy in a society that prizes slimness. Images in the media show stick-thin celebrities and models – but these are people whose lives depend on how they look and have an array of products, services and people to keep them looking 'fabulous'. Comparing yourself to the thin and famous is just going to be a recipe for misery: don't do it.

Unless you like yourself, it is going to be really hard to make the lifestyle changes that will help you lose weight. So try these top tips.

Here's an idea for you ...

Wearing black is 'slimming', but adding touches of colour can really lift your mood: red for energy, blue for communication, yellow for intellectual sharpness and purple for calm.

Get the picture
Develop a more realistic picture of how you would like to look: like you, but in better shape. Then write down all the things you like about yourself, turning them into positive statements and saying them to yourself every day.

Listen to your friends
If that seems too hard, ask your friends or family to write down what they love about you. And if someone pays you a compliment, accept it without putting yourself down.

Exercise
Exercise is good for your self image. Not only will you see physical results, but you'll feel benefits, from the satisfaction of doing something positive for yourself to a greater sense of wellbeing.

What counts
Rather than seeing your body as a collection of parts you think are awful, focus on it as a whole and think of the wonderful things you have done or will do with it. Cuddle someone, run a marathon, climb trees, help old ladies across the road … it's your list, you finish it.

25. Vicious circuits

A complete body workout in the space of a lunch hour? That, in a nutshell, is the appeal of circuit training.

Circuits are a great way to pack in a lot of variety and hard work in a short period of time – like your lunch hour. Variety, because a circuit consists of a dozen or more different exercises which mix and match strength and cardio workouts. Hard work, because knowing that you only have a couple of minutes on each one makes it easier to go for it. A well-organised circuit alternates between strength and cardio, or upper and lower body, so that each station functions as an 'active rest' period for the last. Since stations change according to the whim of the instructors, you may also find yourself trying exercises you wouldn't normally do. See it as a kind of exercise speed dating.

It's theoretically possible to set up a circuit training session on your own using the gym equipment, but Sod's Law says that just as you are about to move on to another piece of equip-ment, someone will start using it for

Here's an idea for you ...

To make press-ups work harder on your back, abs and obliques, off-set your hands so one is a bit forward and the other a bit behind the line of your shoulders.

Defining idea ...

'Leave all the afternoon for exercise and recreation, which are as necessary as reading. I will rather say more necessary because health is worth more than learning.'
THOMAS JEFFERSON

you. See if your gym has an area set aside for circuits for the best, most stress-free work out.

What can I expect?
Typical moves are squats and step-ups (using a bench) to work the lower body, plus crunches and bicycle kicks for the abs. Favourites include press-ups, jumping jacks or burpees. Shuttle runs and skipping help keep the heart rate too. The aim is to do as many repetitions as you can manage during the session. Session lengths may vary but 60 seconds is common and the overall goal is maximum fitness result in minimum time – something we can all relate to.

26. Run like Radcliffe: Fartlek

Stop sniggering. This is how to make the treadmill seem less of a, well, treadmill.

If you're already a gym regular you won't need to be told that, aside from injury, the biggest threat to success is boredom. Worst of all has to be running on the treadmill – itself a byword for tedious routine.

Enter fartlek. All right, all right, settle down at the back there. It's Swedish for speedplay. With fartlek, you vary your pace and effort, rewarding bursts of extra hard work with recovery periods at an easier rate. That's the speed part. The play part comes in by throwing in an element of unpredictability: you run faster as you pass, say, a man with a dog, and do not slow down until you pass a baby-buggy.

Here's an idea for you ...

TVs in gyms are ideal for fartlek. Try to run at above race pace for the duration of the next music video, or until your team slots one into the back of the net.

Defining idea …

'Try increasing the pace of your running between two landmarks as you run; this allows your body to become accustomed to running at a variety of paces.'
PAULA RADCLIFFE

Fartleking around

In the gym there aren't usually a lot of baby-buggies or men with dogs, but you do have a treadmill capable of different speeds and angles of climb. Instead of your normal run, try warming up gently for five minutes then increasing the gradient dramatically for five minutes, or sprinting the next half a kilometre at a speed a good couple of notches up from your usual. As for the element of the unexpected, you usually have a whole gym-full of suspects who can unwittingly be roped in. Try sprinting for as long as the huge guy can manage those bench presses, or rest until the Green Goddess reaches the water fountain. A good session should include a mix of easy running, hard running, hill climbing, walking and absolutely flat out. Just remember: sometimes it's better to call it 'speedplay', not 'fartlek', unless of course you're comfortable about having your would-be admirers collapse into a fit of giggles.

27. I want it and I want it now

Run, hide or play dead and a few other bright ideas to control the food cravings that well up in most of us.

Do cravings represent a nutritional need? The experts still disagree, but there is no doubt that your cravings can be related to what is going on in your body. This seems to be particularly true for women: many women experience strong cravings just before menstruation, or when pregnant. Men don't get so many cravings, and it seems we all grow out of them in the end: the over-65s have fewer cravings than younger people.

The bad news is that people who are trying to lose weight experience the most cravings. Diets that are very restrictive become incredibly dull and banned foods become dispro-portionately attractive. But a healthy, long-term, balanced approach to los-ing weight won't encourage cravings

Here's an idea for you ...

Green tea can raise the metabolic rate. If you drink four or five cups a day, you could burn up around 70 calories – for doing very little!

Defining idea ...

'Food is like sex. When you abstain, even the worst stuff begins to look good.'
BETH McCOLLISTER

because there's no real deprivation. Still, if a craving does sneak up on you like an uninvited guest, try one of these tricks.

■ Bring on a substitute

If it's chocolate you're craving, would a glass of chocolate milk made with skimmed milk do? Try grating a square of chocolate on top. If your lust is for ice-cream, go for a sorbet instead.

■ Pay attention to portion size

Buy a kid's or travel size of your favourite food, just not a family size! Or, measure out a small portion of what you fancy, sit down, take your time and really enjoy it.

■ Give in and don't beat yourself up

Denying yourself a craving could lead to a full-scale binge. But while you eat, see if you can identify a pattern in your cravings, such as times of the day. The more you understand your eating habits, the easier it is to tackle them.

28. Walk yourself thinner

Here's a simple way to drop some weight. It's easy to start, and requires no special clothing or equipment.

There is a good reason to put one foot in front of the other more often. Half an hour's walking will burn up an average of about two hundred calories and help to tone up your legs and bottom. There's just one catch: you won't see results with a gentle stroll to the shops once a week. To make a difference, you'll need to walk at least three times a week, building up to five times a week, for half an hour. You'll need to do it at a reasonable pace, one that warms you up and leaves you feeling slightly breathless, but not so breathless that you could not hold a conversation. If you walk up some hills, you'll increase the challenge and burn up more calories. It is simple. Here are a few other pointers to bear in mind:

Here's an idea for you ...

Don't give up on low-fat dairy products. In research, obese volunteers lost 11% of their body weight over six months on a calorie-controlled diet that included three low-fat dairy portions a day.

Defining idea ...

'Walking is the best possible exercise.'
THOMAS JEFFERSON

■ You'll work harder outdoors than inside on a treadmill as you'll have to cope with changing terrain and wind resistance. This is a good thing as you'll burn calories faster and get extra toning benefits.

■ When walking, keep your tummy muscles pulled in to work your abdominal muscles and protect your back. Walk tall, avoid slumping and use your natural stride.

■ If you swing your arms while you walk, you'll increase your heart rate and get more of a workout.

■ For the best technique, hit the ground with your heel first, roll through your foot and then push off with your toes.

Rather than just randomly walking, try to schedule a daily walk, or at least every other day. That way, you are more likely to stick with it and see results, plus you'll be able to monitor your progress.

29. Keeping your feet on the ground

When it comes to shoes, a proper fit is the key to getting fit.

Most people choose them on either price or brand without a thought to what they're actually going to do. Most 'sports' shoes are completely unsuitable and won't protect you.

Running shoes
When you run, the entire weight of your bounding body comes crashing down on one small part of your foot. One of the key differences between us is the way our feet take the shock – pronation, to the experts. With a neutral footfall the first point of impact is the heel, then your sole, the ball of your foot and your toes. Easy to design a shoe for – if we all had truly neutral footfall. Most of us *overpronate*: our foot lands on the outside edge of the heel and rolls inwards. Others *oversupinate*, rolling their feet outwards. And some of us have strong heelstrike, or strike on the ball. Each requires a different design of shoe to

Here's an idea for you ...

Take your old gym shoes with you when you go to the shop to get advice on a new pair. The way they wear down speaks volumes.

73

Defining idea …

'If you can't fly, then run. If you can't run, then walk. If you can't walk, then crawl. But whatever you do, keep moving.'
MARTIN LUTHER KING, JR

minimise the impact. The answer? Get thee to a specialist running shop for someone can see you run and suggest shoes to suit.

Cross-trainers
Running shoes are great for running – but running is just one kind of motion. Unless you're a very unusual runner, your feet will always be moving forwards, whereas the moment you indulge in martial arts, step or just about any other training you will start moving sideways, jumping and changing direction suddenly. Now your foot needs lateral cushioning. So if you can't resist those step classes, you'd do better to get a dedicated cross-trainer.

The golden rule is to buy the shoe to suit the job its going to do, not to suit the suits in the marketing department

30. Row like Redgrave

Rowing can be great for your core strength, but why do so many users look less like Steve Redgrave and more like Mr Bean?

Rowing is right up there with swimming as one of the best all-round exercises you can do – but with the handy difference that you don't have to navigate shrieking ten-year-olds at half term and you're unlikely to end up with a nose full of chlorinated pee. Done properly, rowing is a great calorie burner, combining weight control with strength development and a cardio workout. Do it badly, however, and you end up staggering away from the machine bent over double.

Pros break the action down into four distinct movements:

Here's an idea for you …

Few of us really understand resistance levels at all – most blokes whack the lever up to 10 in case anyone should think they're not Olympic heroes. Real Olympic heroes tend to go for the feel that is most like a real boat (a level of 3 or 4 according to Terry O'Neill, former Olympic rowing coach), then aim for about 35 strokes a minute.

The catch

You're sitting on the rower and your feet are safely strapped in. Slide forward so your shins are vertical, the handle in both hands with your wrists flat and your torso leaning slightly forwards from the hips.

The drive

The powerhouse for this is the legs, never the arms. So straighten those legs, pushing hard against the foot rests, and keep the arms straight for the first part of the drive. As your legs straighten, your arms start to bend slightly and your upper body comes into play, leaning slightly backwards.

The finish

Legs straighten completely, upper body leans lightly backwards, and you pull the handle in towards your stomach just below your rib cage. At the end of the pull your elbows should be tucked in close to your body and behind your back, not sticking out sideways.

The recovery

The arms extend forwards, then your upper body leans lightly forward, and your legs bend as you slide smoothly back towards the flywheel down by your feet.

Get rowing right and not only do you reduce soreness and the risk of injury, but you will effortlessly increase both your speed and endurance.

31. High (calorie) spirits

Sociable, mood-enhancing, delicious ... but alcohol can also be ruinous to your waistline.

The trouble with alcohol is that one glass so easily leads to another. Or four.

Know your units

The UK recommended guidelines for alcohol consumption are 21 units for men and 14 for women. What's a unit? Always disappointingly small, I think – a half pint of beer, a small (125 ml) glass of wine and a single measure (25 ml) of spirits. Interestingly, doctors reckon that people underestimate their alcohol consumption by 50%, which is why it's a good idea to record your intake over a period of a few weeks to assess if you need to make some changes.

Here's an idea for you ...

If you're eating out, skip the aperitifs. As well as cutting back a few calories, you'll have a clear head when you come to order. Alcohol can have a strange way of making deep fried camembert look like the perfect choice!

Defining idea ...

Alcohol and diet

Alcohol is full of calories, but not much else (it has few nutrients to boast about). To lose a pound a week, you need to cut 500 calories a day – and as a strong lager can clock up 350 calories, you see why cutting down on alcohol makes sense. Then there's the fact that alcohol seems to make you snack. How quickly handfuls of peanuts and crisps slip down when you're enjoying a few cocktails! There's no doubt that alcohol weakens the resolve too, so resolve to keep it under control.

Be a lite drinker

There are less fattening choices of drinks of course. Try a white wine spritzer instead of a (175 ml) glass of wine, i.e. use half the amount of wine and top up with soda, and you save half the calories. Strong lagers are usually twice as high in calories as ordinary strength lagers. Slimline or diet mixers will also help to reduce the calorific impact of tipples such as vodka and tonic.

32. The morning after the night before

Weddings, birthdays, anniversaries, new job, new home – they are all great excuses for a party and could lead you into temptation.

It's hard to resist free-flowing alcohol and high-calorie snacks and treats in a happy, loud atmosphere. How easily those handfuls of peanuts can slip down. More wine? How about a cocktail? Have a slice of cake. The next thing you know, you've completely overdone it.

Come the morning, you wake up feeling bloated, cross and disappointed in yourself. Your reaction could be to give up. Don't. Instead of dwelling on the results of your over indulgence, say to yourself 'I've been losing weight steadily and after my break yesterday, I'm confident and eager to get back to my healthy habits today'. And you can learn from your experience too. Which foods in

Here's an idea for you ...

Play with plate size. If you eat from an enormous plate, chances are you'll fill it with an enormous portion or feel short-changed because there doesn't appear to be much on it! Choosing a smaller plate and piling it up is a sneaky way to trick yourself that you're having a big meal.

Defining idea …

'When I read about the evils of
drinking, I gave up reading.'
HENNY YOUNGMAN

particular couldn't you get enough of?
Was it the alcohol that was your down-
fall? Did you continue to eat when you
felt full? Identifying the pitfalls will
help with the next party.

As for feeling tired the morning after the night before, you need
some damage-limitation tricks. Chances are you'll be craving carbohydrates to boost your energy levels and, if you're hungover, fatty foods
too. Start the day with a large glass of water to combat dehydration,
then have a slow-energy release breakfast – porridge, a slice of
wholemeal toast or a smoothie. Drink another couple of glasses of
water and, if you need to snack, eat fruit, crackers or a rice cake. A
huge salad with low-fat protein for lunch, then an early evening meal
of grilled fish or meat with plenty of vegetables should sort you out.
Early to bed and tomorrow you'll feel fab.

33. Alternatives to kaftans

Being groomed and stylish is important whether you're just starting out on your weight loss plan or already beginning to change shape.

Not so long ago, unless you were a 'size tiny', all that was on offer was a tent, kaftan or baggy tracksuit. Manufacturers have at last woken up to the fact that people come in all shapes and sizes, and we all want to look good.

The extraordinary amount of choice on the High Street now means that, whatever your budget or measurements, you'll be able to look good (which makes you feel good too). Here are some tips for dressing well and looking slimmer.

For men

■ Avoid jackets with extra padding, and shapeless jumpers – they'll make you look bulkier.

Here's an idea for you ...

Go through your wardrobe and throw away anything that is baggy and shapeless or too tight. Try on dodgy items and take a long, hard look in the mirror. Any doubts, chuck it out.

Defining idea …

- Go for trousers and jacket in the same colour to streamline.
- Single-breasted jackets are more slimming than double-breasted.
- Buy the right size! Anything cling-ing over a large belly looks slobby.
- Go for looser fits and ensure that you can do your trousers up somewhere near you waist.
- A V-neck is especially good if you have a large neck.

For women
- Don't wear your tops tucked in. Try a chunky low-slung belt worn over a loose top.
- An A-line skirt is great for hiding big thighs and bottoms.
- Combat and narrow trousers maximise every curve. Try a boot leg cut or flares.
- Beware anything that is too small, including underwear – you will just bulge out.
- Go for fabrics that drape, such as cotton and jerseys as opposed to fabrics that cling, such as satin and Lycra.
- Leggings and other Lycra trousers and shorts should be kept for the gym.

34. Lunch boxes

What's in your lunch box today? Breakfast might be the most important meal of the day, but you shouldn't ignore lunch.

The high-paced pressure of modern life means that lunch is often forgotten. You've been working throughout the day only to find that, when you finally stop for a break, it's suppertime. It's a tragedy so many people miss out on lunch – and usually snack on foods that offer short-term rewards, but are unkind to your waistline.

Working lunches that don't work
Even if you do have some lunch there's a good chance it will be a working one, in a meeting room, with a plate of wilting sandwiches, some burning brown beverage and a jug of burn-soothing water. At least you may get a little pleasure from lunch this way, rather than sitting in front of the computer, juggling a sandwich and drink as you try to type, move the mouse or talk on the phone.

Here's an idea for you ...

Set a time when you and your colleagues have lunch together, if possible have it away from the working area or outside.

Defining idea …

'My body is like breakfast, lunch, and dinner. I don't think about it, I just have it.'
ARNOLD SCHWARZENEGGER

On a roll

Lunches on the go are going up too. Pacing from one meeting to the next, on your mobile with a crusty roll stuffed in your mouth. You will not be able to digest it properly, and what you are eating is probably extremely unhealthy too. Full of saturated fat, salt and calories …

Sign up to better lunches

You've seen the phrase 'out to lunch'. It used to appear in shop windows. And no, it didn't mean that the person was a few sandwiches short of a picnic. It meant that they had actually gone out to lunch. You can too. You don't need a sign, although you could make one if it helps. Just leaving your workstation, switching off your mobile phone, and spending half an hour having lunch will leave you refreshed and efficient on your return – and create a healthier eating habit along the way.

35. In the swim

Swimming is one of the best all-round exercises, but most of us are no better than we were at school. Learn to cut a dash as you splash.

Swimming involves your whole body – including your abs – increasing strength, flexibility and endurance with little risk of injury. But it can be hard to make progress. The default is to flounder up and down the same as ever, but you won't improve. If a coach is not an option, here are some exercises you can do for yourself. At the very least they will make a change from the end-to-end plodding.

Break it down
Whatever your favourite stroke, it co-ordinates arm and leg actions – but to get better, you're going to have to get uncoordinated, just for the moment. Focus on: just the arm, then just the leg.

Floats and pull-buoys
Remember the humble float from school? The pull-buoy is just a float shaped so it's easier to hold between

Here's an idea for you ...

Swim a length and count the number of strokes it takes. Now using what you've learnt from swimming with arms or legs only try to swim the length using fewer strokes. The fewer, the better.

Defining idea ...

*'Fitness is something that happens
to you while you're practising good
technique.'*
**TERRY LAUGHLIN, swim coach
and director of the total
immersion school of swimming**

your legs. If your pool doesn't have
any, a normal float will do – it'll just try
harder to get away from you.

Legs

Scissors kick, butterfly kick or frog leg
strokes should all be enough to propel
you from one end of the pool to the
other. Grab a float, hold it out with both hands and use only your legs
to swim.

Arms

As with legs, only in reverse. Lodge a pull buoy or a float (two, if you
need) between your thighs. Now set off up the pool using only your
arm stroke.

Don't aim for speed, just for comfort. If you are tired after a length,
try putting less effort into the stroke, and getting more out by means
of better form.

36. Members only

Slimming clubs promise results, but will they make more of a dent in your pocket than your fat reserves?

Millions of people the world over belong to slimming organisations. Although the majority of clubbers are female, men are signing up too. But is a club the right place for you? Try these for starters:

1. Is there any evidence that this club's methods work? Ask for testimonials and press clippings.
2. What are the costs and payment structure? Will you have to pay for any extras?
3. How convenient will the meetings be for you, both in terms of time and geography? Are there options to follow the programme on-line or by post?
4. What are the club rules? Does it focus solely on diet, and if so, what are the basic guidelines you will follow? Is exercise included in sessions or recommended?

Here's an idea for you …

Worried that people might be too competitive? Sometimes a little competition isn't a bad thing. Maybe you should take some support along with you – a friend or your partner, for instance.

Defining idea ...

'I have a mind to join a club and beat you over the head with it.'
GROUCHO MARX

5   What would a typical day's menu look like? Better to find out now!

6   When you reach your target weight, do they offer a maintenance plan? Does it cost extra?

7   Can you sit in on a session to see what it's like?

As well as the big name diet clubs, your local doctor or hospital may well run a weight-loss programme, and your local gym may offer one too. And don't be conned by the super-fast weight loss hucksters. Seductive as it might seem, losing a vast amount of weight quickly is not sustainable. It will be water and lean muscle mass that disappears, only to reappear when you start to live normally again. If you try to do it with some unproven diet pill you could be putting yourself in all kinds of other health dangers, too. Go for the tried and tested methods.

37. Snooze and lose

**What has sleep got to do with
weight loss? Get your pyjamas on.
I'll tuck you in and explain.**

The notion of sleep as a powerful aid to wellbe-
ing makes sense. As well as giving your body time to recharge, a good
sleep makes you feel on top of the world. But research in the US has
also revealed that people who don't get enough sleep are more likely
to go for high-sugar, high-fat foods and drink. And if you're not getting enough sleep on a prolonged basis, it could interfere with your
body's ability to metabolise carbohydrates by up to 40%, according to
another US study.

While we're asleep, our brains go from light through to deep sleep, on
to Rapid Eye Movement (REM) sleep.
Experts generally agree that bodily
repair happens in deep sleep and brain
repair during REM sleep, but disrup-
tion of REM sleep has been found to
lead to an increase in appetite.

Here's an idea for you ...

Choose black coffee. A large full-fat
latte packs in a hefty 260 calories. Or
opt for a cappuccino with skimmed
milk, for just 100 calories.

Defining idea ...

'Farly to bed and early to rise makes a man healthy, wealthy and wise.'
BENJAMIN FRANKLIN

How much sleep do you need?
It varies. Most of us sleep for between six and ten hours, with the average around eight. Whatever leaves you refreshed and full of energy is right for you. The quality of your sleep counts too. Here are some ways to maximise it:

- Keep your bedroom for sleeping – no work, eating or TV (which encourage snacking).
- Alcohol and caffeine are best avoided before bedtime. Tossing and turning can leave you hungry for snacks the next day.
- Keep to regular bed and waking times. Forget weekend lie-ins: they interfere with your body's natural rhythm.
- If your partner snores, try earplugs.
- When your mind races or, visualise yourself putting your worries in a drawer and locking it, telling yourself you'll deal with it in the morning.
- Make yourself a warm drink of milk (skimmed, of course). There's no real proof this helps but it's very comforting.

38. Burn baby burn

Eating less and working out harder will result in weight loss. Simple.

The secret to burning fat faster is to maximise the fat-burning potential of everything you do, including the routines you've slipped into as you work out. Here are three tips to use at home or in the gym.

Lighter, but longer
If the prospect of an intense workout at the gym or a 15 km hike around your local park horrifies you, try working out less fast, but for longer. For example, walking briskly for an hour burns the same amount of calories as running for half an hour.

Build some muscle
Use weights, either on gym machines, in a workout class or as part of a home fitness routine. This will help you burn fat and not just because simply lifting weights uses energy. Pumping iron (I know, it's such a male term, but women, please take note) builds

Here's an idea for you …

Following a workout, your body experiences an 'after-burn', replacing short-term energy loss with energy from your fat stores. After an hour, go for a protein and carbohydrate snack, like a tuna and salad sandwich.

Defining idea …

'My idea of exercise is a good brisk
sit.'
PHYLLIS DILLER

muscle tissue, which is metabolically
more active that fat tissue. Muscle uses
more energy than fat just to exist, so
the more muscle you have, the more
calories get used, even when you're
resting.

Learn to love intervals
I don't mean going off mid-performance to have an ice-cream or
a glass of wine; I mean interval training. The idea is that you can
increase the amount of calories you burn during any exercise by
increasing the speed, intensity or duration, even for brief intervals.
If you are walking, swimming or cycling, go steady for about 15–20
minutes, then faster for a couple of minutes, then slow down again
and speed up in random bursts.

Remember, the fitter you are, the better your body becomes at using
its fuel, which translates into a leaner, more toned you. And the more
exercise you do, the quicker you'll see results.

39. Designer labels

It has a little healthy eating logo on it, so it must be good for you, right? No! Learn to read labels and help yourself lose weight.

What do those labels on all your food products really mean? Here's a start.

- RDA

    This is the recommended daily amount published by the government and calculated to prevent nutritional deficiency in at least 95% of people. You can check the RDA against calories, fat, protein, and so on.

- Lite/light

    There are no real rules to say how much fat and calories should be in something that describes itself this way. Check the nutritional label yourself against a standard, i.e. non light, version, using the per 100g breakdown. Light in fat can still contain as many calories as

Here's an idea for you …

Check your loaf. The fat content of a slice of bread can vary from around 60 calories a slice with 0.9 g of fat, to 115 calories a slice with 2.7g of fat and even more!

a standard product because sugar has been added to compensate for example.

■ Low fat/fat free

By law you can't be misled on this one. The UK Food Standards Agency suggests that 'low fat' should only be claimed when the fat content is less than 3g per 100g. 'Fat-free' should be for foods that only have a trace of fat – under 0.15mg per 100g. Beware anything that says '90% fat-free' – that means it's still 10% fat!

■ Reduced fat

Sounds good, but the recommendation is that it can only appear on foods that have less than three quarters of the amount of fat of the standard product. Again, check against the original product. Reduced fat taramasalata dip, for example, still contains 25 g fat per 100 g. So it's better than regular taramasalata, but not necessarily the best choice of dip.

Finally, beware 'healthy eating' logos. Often when fat is reduced, fillers are used for bulk, and the sugar and salt contents may be high too. Maybe the calories are reduced because it's a tiny portion! Compare, compare, compare!

40. Good morning Superman

Working hard for a flat stomach but neglecting your back muscles? Don't. You'll end up like Quasimodo.

It's one of the simplest but smartest features of our body that most muscles have an opposite muscle that's just as important. Where one pulls, the other pushes. Most exercises are designed to work both, so as not to create an imbalance. In one key area, however, that rule seems to go out of the window. We spend a lot of time worrying about rock-hard bellies, but forget that unless we strengthen the spinal muscles to cope we could be sowing the seeds of serious back trouble.

The erector spinae muscles run up the length of the spine and help straighten the back. The more you're working the rest of your body, the more you need to work these to hold it all together. Just one thing though. Before working

Here's an idea for you ...

Try doing a Superman on a Swiss ball. With your feet firmly on the floor, lie face down on the ball so it supports your stomach. Lift your head and shoulders off the ball and curve your back upwards.

your back, you should get qualified medical advice and talk to a gym instructor. Promise? OK, over to you.

Superman – or indeed Superwoman
Lie flat on your front on a mat and smoothly lift both your arms and your feet off the mat as if you were trying to curl your whole body into a bow shape with only your stomach, ribs and hips left on the mat. Keep it steady, hold it for a moment, then return. Now add a slight twist to that by slowly raising your right arm with your left leg, then your left arm with your right leg. This should be comfortable enough to do ten or twenty times without feeling difficulty.

Take a bow
Stand with your feet shoulder-width apart and your knees slightly bent. Bend forward from the waist until your torso is parallel to the floor and hold before gently rising back up. Bravo.

41. Gettin' jiggy in the gym

Music may or may not be the food of love but it certainly makes the time fly when you're performing the flywheel fandango on rowers or exercise bikes.

Gyms and music

Gyms and music have always gone together, but the results are sometimes less Torvill and Dean, more Laurel and Hardy. The thing is, it's got to be the *right* music. If it's music you want to pay attention to, you may not be paying enough attention to your exercises. So leave that Schubert sonata or whale song at home, and go for something energetic, rousing and definitely more about beat than lyrics.

Most gyms have canned music – useless for rhythm since it's half drowned out by the machines. Many have radio or TV channels but you'll quickly learn that even 'dance' channels seem to be about fifty per cent talk. Which isn't

Here's an idea for you ...

When you record your compilation take note of how long each song is. Next time you're on a cardio machine, just keep going for a set number of songs – five, ten, whatever. Time will fly.

Defining idea …

'You are the music while the music lasts.'
T. S. ELLIOT

what you want as you try to attain that trance-like out-of-body feeling.

Bring your own
BYO music is the answer. Make your own compilation of upbeat energy. Plenty of people make up their favourite party compilations; why do so few put the same effort into jazzing up the gym session? Your choice will help put some spice into your next session. Guaranteed.

Wanna play?
Which leaves the question of how to play your personal soundtrack.

MP3 players have to be loaded up with music via a computer but they are cute, small and won't miss a beat; mobile phones often feature MP3 players or FM radios; CD Walkmen are cheap and cheerful, but can skip; MiniDiscs are easy to record to – they just plug into your hi-fi; and hard-drive jukeboxes (think Apple iPod or the Creative Labs' Jukebox Zen) hold gigabytes of data, shuffle tracks, find that elusive track … in fact, for aficionados, the hard-drive jukebox is the Holy Grail.

42. Timesaving tips

Too pressed for time for tons of presses? In fact, little and often is better than sporadic blitzing. Try a few of these tips to maximise those fleeting moments in the gym.

Only a few precious minutes to spare? Here's how you can get a decent workout super fast.

Get packing
Einstein used to line up seven sets of clothes each week so he never wasted precious brainpower. Get smart. When you pull stuff out of the dryer, match it up, pack it and leave it sitting by the door. Sorted.

Plan your workout, work your plan
Nobody has enough time at the gym, so who are all those people wandering around aimlessly? Be clear in advance how much cardio you want to do or what weight session you have in mind.

Here's an idea for you ...

Don't wait for your favourite machine to be free. Use the opportunity to discover something else. You just might like it!

Defining idea ...

'That's so when I forget how to spell my name, I can still find my clothes.'
STU GRIMSON, American football player, explaining why he has a photograph of himself on his locker

Go early

What? Like in the morning? Working out before the day gets its claws into you means you feel good and your metabolism's up and running. You'll feel so virtuous you might even come back tomorrow.

Train with the ones you love

Mix gym/social life by training with friends and family. Swap your abs class for something more fun, like a core class, and you can frolic with the whole family.

Don't rest, cross-train

Your gym says no more than 20 minutes on a machine? Fine, just leap straight onto another one. Take ten on each for a more thorough workout. You'll put in more effort if you know you're changing soon too.

Don't rest, superset

Instead of resting for 30 seconds between sets, switch straight to an exercise that works the opposite set of muscles. If you're working biceps, alternate with a triceps press; pair chest press exercises with lateral pull downs; hamstrings with quads, etc.

43. Mortal combat

Mixing martial arts moves and music is a trend sweeping gyms world-wide. Work off some aggression while you shed some pounds.

Skipping around beating the hell out of thin air might not sound like an appropriate pastime for a grown adult but it's a rare gym these days that doesn't feature body combat, tae box or another exotically named equivalent. Perhaps they're a sign of these stressful times, a tribute to the subtle artistry of Jean Claude Van Damme. Whatever. The fact is that for a lot of people aggressive workouts work.

BodyCombat is the trademark name of the workout from the Les Mills company (the guys who brought you BodyPump) and if your gym isn't a subscriber, then it will probably have another flavour with a different name but much the same moves. The moves are taken from boxing, tai chi, kickboxing and tae kwondo, choreo-

Here's an idea for you ...

Ask at your gym if any of the courses with martial arts moves actually involve contact pads, then trot along and try it. You still warm up by heaving punches and launching kicks at the atmosphere, but you then move on to trying to land them on someone. This isn't as painful as it sounds. You'll be divided up into pairs and one of you holds the pad while the other launches attacks on it.

Defining idea ...

graphed into all-dancing, all-kicking extravaganzas. As well as delivering a great cardio workout, they are often trumpeted as 'empowering' – but don't get carried away and try to quell pub fights with your fabulous air kicks.

Mortal arts are billed as non-contact but that doesn't mean they are no-impact for your body. The bouncing up and down, sudden changes of direction and shooting your limbs out in various directions are all exhilarating but hard on the joints. You'll need to be in fairly good shape, and wearing shoes with good ankle support.

Make contact
In this field, the thing that separates the men from the boys/women from the girls is contact. Ask at your gym if any of the courses with martial arts moves actually involve contact pads, then trot along and try it. You'll still start by heaving punches at the atmosphere, but then you'll land them on someone – with pads for protection, of course.

44. What's the next big thing?

Heard about the glycemic index? The GI Diet or one of its relatives could be the one for you.

At last. A diet that's easy to follow and live with. It works for vegetarians, too. The GI diet is basically pretty healthy and people achieve great results with it. So what's it about?

Originally developed during research for diabetes, the glycemic index is a measure of how quickly you digest various foods and convert them into your body's energy source: glucose. Glucose, or sugar, is rated at 100 and everything else gets scored against that. So cornflakes come in at 84, for example, while oatmeal is 42. Eating low GI foods means you're satisfied for longer, while those with high ratings on the index not only make you feel hungry again quicker (cue snacking), but also trigger off various processes that lead to fat formation and fat storage.

Here's an idea for you ...

Some forward-thinking supermarkets are starting to label products with a low GI and medium GI rating. For a list of over 500 of these, visit www.tesco.com and look at their GI section.

Defining idea ...

'I decided to try this diet. To my amazement and delight I lost the twenty pounds that had been plaguing me for so long.'
RICK GALLOP, author of the GI Diet

However, that's not the whole picture. The GI Diet, to take one of my favourites (by Rick Gallop), also promotes eating a combination of low GI foods that are low in sugar and fat, therefore calories too. Foods are rated red light – avoid; amber – eat occasionally; and green – as much as you want.

So for example, at breakfast, it's yes to whole fruit, low-fat yoghurt, some cereals and even a bit of toast (no butter, mind). You can't have sausages or regular bacon, but a bit of leaner back bacon or lean ham is fine. No to muffins and croissants, but yes to porridge. And you can have coffee too – just as long as it's the decaffeinated sort, because caffeine increases insulin production and reduces blood sugar levels, making you hungry.

45. Squat yet bijoux

Don't leave squats to the powerlifters. This simple move can firm up your middle too.

With attention to form, squats can work your abs and obliques and protect your back from the wear and tear of daily life. So much from so little. Yet most of us believe they are best left to vast, pumped-up East Europeans.

The main reasons why people shy away from squats are:

- Fear of provoking back trouble.
- Fear of ending up looking like a powerlifter.
- They're hard.
- They are the opposite of glamour – even the name is ugly.

OK, the last point is a fair cop, but the whole point of the gym thing is how you look outside, not while you're in there. As for the others they all seem to presume that you're going to squat

Here's an idea for you ...

Make like a sleeping flamingo by doing a one-legged squat. This asks even more of the stabilising muscles of your joints and your mid-section. Just raise one leg so that the thigh is parallel with the floor and slowly lower your body as far as you can. Repeat with the other leg.

Defining idea ...

'The back squat should be regarded as the most useful free-weights exercise.'
Hardgainer Magazine

with weights the size of car wheels on each end of the bar. The basic squat can be done with nothing more than your own bodyweight if you prefer, adding a barbell when you're ready.

Use your bodyweight
Start with your feet shoulder-width apart, legs lightly bent at the knee. Breathe in and pull your shoulders back so your spine assumes its natural curve. With your arms out like a sleepwalker, ease yourself down as if sitting into an armchair. If you lift onto the balls of your feet, you are unbalanced forwards. Keep the whole sole of your foot firmly planted on the floor.

Once you're comfortable doing squats without weight, try the 'broomstick' held across the back of your shoulders. Happy with three sets of 12 reps with the stick? Time to move to the barbell.

46. In the kitchen

Equip your kitchen so you can cook up low fat food in healthy ways. Then use it.

Cupboard love

- Store healthy foods like high-fibre flour, pasta and dried fruit. Chuck out the refined foods, like bags of sugar, cake mix or biscuits.

- Go for non-stick pans: you won't need so much fat to cook with them. Pans for stir-frying need a little more fat, but the quick cooking method preserves the goodness in your food. Steamers are also great –no hidden calories when you cook up your vegetables or fish in these.

- Gravy boats should have a funnel arrangement to siphon off the fat, while preserving all the flavour.

- And, fingers crossed, there'll be no fat fryer or sandwich toaster. Any snacks you cook in these will be loaded.

Here's an idea for you ...

Use your kitchen scales to check the real weight of the portions you're eating. A little bit could make a big difference, and you could be fooling yourself, so don't guess.

Defining idea …

'The first step to getting the things you want out of life is this: decide what you want.'
BEN STEIN, US writer and broadcaster

Counter culture

- Your worktop should be busy, with plenty of evidence of home cooking. Perhaps a bowl too, full to the brim of tantalising fruit for your five-a-day quota.

- Bread-machine? Fine, as so long as the bread that emerges is not over-dense. If it is, you'll end up eating twice as much bulk – and therefore more carbohydrate and calories – than with commercially prepared bread.

- What's around the kettle? A range of options for healthy hot drinks? Look for low-calorie clear soups, decaf and herbal tea, and for cold drinks, strictly no-sugar models. No cordials or drinking chocolate, thank you very much.

- And bless the microwave. It's going to let your home-prepared frozen meals spring to life, and save you from junky ready meals when you're starving. It'll cook up food without adding fat too. Why not find out how to use it?

47. Skip it

Small girls know that skipping is fun. Big boxers know that skipping is really tough. Somewhere in between, there's something for you.

Skipping is a huge calorie burner – for a 75 kg man think about 750 calories per hour. It gives much of the workout of running with far less impact. And it doesn't require waiting in line for a treadmill either.

Look for a rope with foam handles and a plastic rope – from £5 to £20 at a sports shop near you.

Safety

I know, I know, safety issues may seen relative when you're talking about the favourite sport of schoolgirls but they probably don't have all that adult weight you're carrying.

■ Ensure the rope is the right size. When you're standing in the middle, each end should reach your armpits. If it's too long, knot it; if it's too short, get another.

Here's an idea for you ...

Try a boxer's workout. Alternate three-minute skips with a minute of crunches or press-ups, for half an hour.

Defining idea ...

*'Jelly on a plate, jelly on a plate,
wibble wobble, wibble wobble, jelly
on a plate.'*
Traditional

- Make sure you're wearing cross-trainers, not running shoes.
- Stretch before you skip.
- Try to avoid skipping on concrete or a wooden floor that's laid directly on concrete. Use mats.

Getting going
The basic skip step is the pogo with both feet bouncing off the ground together as the rope passes under. Make sure you've got good rhythm or you'll wind up as a red-faced tangle of rope and blasphemy.

Aim for short bursts of 20 seconds then a brief break (a good time to stretch) and repeat. Build up slowly until you can skip for five minutes or more straight. The try some fancy footwork:

- Side swing – Swing the rope to the side of you so it taps the ground, then jump as normal, then swing the rope to the other side.
- Cross jumps – As the rope comes over your head, cross your hands and jump through the rope. then uncross as the rope comes over your head again.

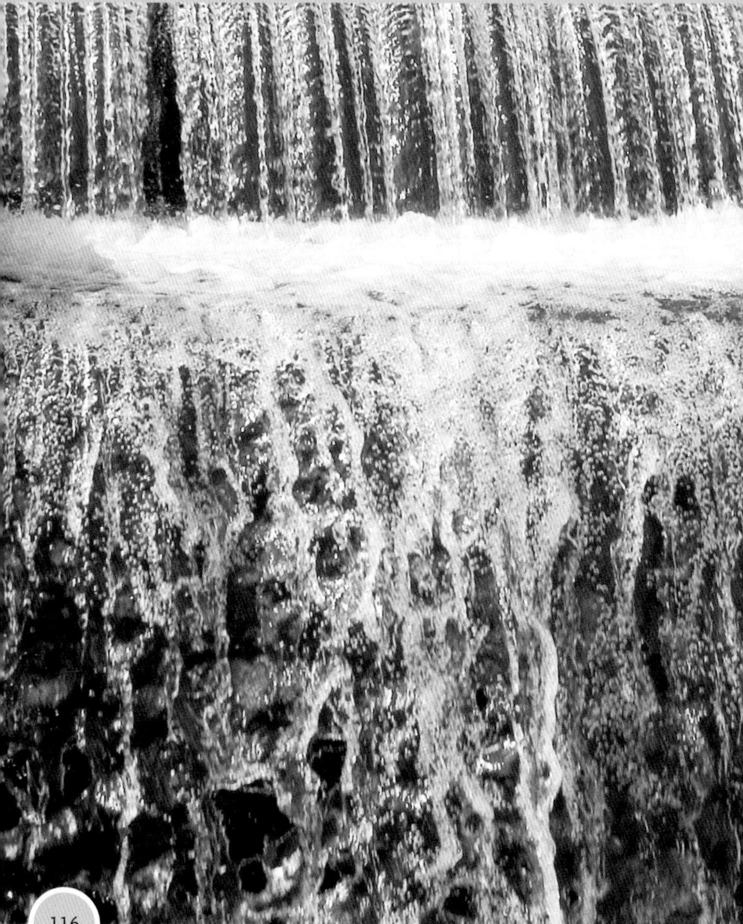

48. Water works

Most of us live in a state of dehydration most of the time. Discover the benefits of drinking more water for your diet.

Water basics

Experts reckon that we need one and a half litres of fluid a day to stay healthy, more if it's hot or if you're sweating. It is hard to drink too much water, but quite easy to not drink enough. Drinking too little water for an extended period can lead to urinary tract infections, kidney and gall stones, as well as headaches, a lack of energy and poor concentration. But if you're looking to lose weight, water can have a further, crucial role to play …

Water and food

About a third of daily fluid intake comes from food, not from liquid. Fruit and vegetables generally supply the most water – for instance, salad leaves are mostly water. Our bodies also get water by burning fats and carbohydrates.

Here's an idea for you …

Your crockery could be influencing your appetite. A US study revealed that bold, bright patterns stimulate your hunger, while pastel hues decrease it. Strange, but true.

Don't eat, drink!

A feeling of thirst indicates that you are already dehydrated. Thirst is a signal that there is a water deficiency in the cells. Often we interpret this feeling as hunger, so we eat rather than drink. This leads quite easily to an unnecessary intake of calories! A large glass or two of water containing zero calories will sort out those 'am I hungry?' feelings.

Stop the spiral

It's important to remember the dehydration spiral: you haven't drunk enough water so you feel hungry and tired, so you snack, but it doesn't make you feel better because you're thirsty, so you eat more before realising you need fluids. Then you feel guilty because you've been snacking, so you snack some more. It's a spiral into more guilt and bad food choices. Break the spiral by drinking frequently, whether or not you think you're thirsty. Eight glasses of water a day is a good target. Take one before and after every meal, and one mid-morning and mid-afternoon.

49. This time it's personal

Personal trainers – fashion accessory or failsafe route to fitness?

Let's be clear about what a personal trainer means. We're not talking about having someone knock up a tailored training routine for you when you first start at the gym – all gyms should do that as a matter of course. Personal trainers will dedicate themselves to you and you alone for each hour that you book. They should assess your fitness level, set up a program complete with goals and waypoints, and provide the motivation to achieve them. If you're thinking of opting for personal training, ensure that the trainer:

- Has a recognised personal trainer qualification.
- Is a member of the Register of Fitness Professionals.
- Has a valid CPR (cardio-pulmonary resuscitation) certificate.

Here's an idea for you …

If you can't afford a personal trainer, try an online personal trainer. Try GymUser (www.gymuser.co.uk), HandBag (www.handbag.com), or www.onlinepersonaltrainer.co.uk.

Defining idea …

Recognised qualifications (as defined by the Register of Fitness Professionals) include:

■ Future Fit Training Personal Trainer
■ YMCA Personal Trainer Diploma
■ Lifetime HF Personal Trainer
■ FIE Certified Personal Trainer
■ Premier Training Diploma
■ A BA-level degree in sports and fitness.

Why pay the extra?
Unsure of your goals? Motivation a big problem? Going nowhere and don't know what to try? Then a personal trainer could be exactly what the doctor ordered.

What can I expect?
If your aim is to lose weight and tone up, then you can expect to start off with a cardio warm-up before going onto weights and moves that you wouldn't normally do. In the process you will learn a lot about form, posture, technique and the use of different pieces of equipment. It also makes the gym session a commitment that you can't back out of, and introduces the trainer as a kind of external conscience nagging you if you let things slip. Sort of like Jiminy Cricket in tracksuit bottoms.

50. Stuck on those last 7 lb?

It's such a small amount, you'd think it would leave without a whimper. But no, that half a stone always seems to be trickiest to shift.

Who knows why, but to make it go away you have to have more tricks up your sleeve than a magician. Well, ten, at least.

1   Be honest with yourself. Keep a food diary for a week and note down everything that you consume.
2   Don't eat large amounts of anything. Even healthy diet-friendly foods such as fruits have calories.
3   Be consistent. Relaxing your rules from time to time is fine, but having a total blow-out every weekend will stack up and your healthful efforts will be for nothing.
4   Be more active, whatever your current levels of activity, to rev up your rate of weight loss.

Here's an idea for you ...

Too many choices can make you eat more. Research has shown that volunteers ate 44% more than a control group when offered a variety of dishes rather than the same amount of one dish.

Defining idea ...

'It's OK to let yourself go, just as long as you let yourself back.'
Mick Jagger

5 Cut out carbohydrates with your evening meal for a couple of weeks, or every other night if that's more convenient. You'll see a difference on the scales.

6 Have healthy snacks between healthy meals. You won't ever feel ravenously hungry, so you're less likely to binge or overeat.

7 Spice up your life with a few hot peppers in your lunch or dinner. Pepper eaters have less of an appetite and feel full quicker according to Canadian research.

8 Include calcium in your diet: it seems to help your body burn excess fat faster.

9 Get your rest. Sleep deprivation and a stressed-out lifestyle can boost levels of cortisol in your body, which is associated with higher levels of insulin and fat storage.

10 Don't eat when you're not hungry. It seems obvious, but next time you put your food in your mouth, ask yourself 'Am I really hungry?' before that second mouthful.

51. What's your excuse?

We all have them – perfectly good reasons why our gut is still there. Only they're not reasons, they're excuses.

Whether they are plausible reasons or fictional tales worthy of Hollywood's finest, the trouble with excuses is that they are stopping you from achieving your goals. Usually there are some powerful emotions struggling underneath these excuses. If you can unravel what they are, it could help you to move on.

'I don't have time to exercise.'
Is your life really so different to people who do exercise? If it's childcare that's an issue, could your partner or neighbour watch the kids? Perhaps you could get up earlier or work out at lunchtime.

Here's an idea for you ...

An interesting US study suggests that eating carbohydrates before you exercise could reduce the amount of fat you burn for hours afterwards. Have a handful of nuts before your workout instead.

123

Defining idea …

'People are always blaming circumstances for what they are. I do not believe in circumstances. The people who get on in this world are the people who get up and look for the circumstances they want, and if they cannot find them, make them.'
GEORGE BERNARD SHAW

'Everyone puts on weight as they get older.'
It's not inevitable, unless you consistently overeat whilst being inactive.

'I don't feel like exercising.'
If you need motivation, make a commitment to working out with a friend or group. If you don't feel like it because you don't like exercise, try something new. You might go for classes, sports, swimming, salsa dancing, martial arts …

'Exercise hurts!'
If it hurts so much you hate it, get dizzy or exhausted, stop. However, if you simply feel some muscle soreness afterwards, it is normal – assuming you warmed up, cooled down and didn't actually injure yourself. The key is not to overdo things. As you get fitter – and you'll see results in a few weeks – you can push yourself harder.

'I just end up bingeing on all the foods I can't have.'
Well, don't deny yourself anything. Have a small amount of your craved food as soon as you want it.

52. Zen and the art of weight loss maintenance

We can all lose weight, at least in the short term, but the greatest challenge is keeping it off.

There's an often-quoted figure that 90% of people who lose weight put it all back on within a year. Rather than dwelling on the reasons for this 'failure', try to figure out how the people who have lost weight and kept it off have done it. Here are the five top reasons:

Strategy 1
People who keep weight off link their positive healthy behaviours with other areas of their lives. For instance, eating sensibly not only helps your health and weight, but it could set a good example to children. Exercise becomes not simply physical activity, but also

Here's an idea for you ...

Successful dieters don't say 'When I lose weight, I'll take that holiday/get a new job/sort out my love life.' They just carry on with living alongside losing weight. So don't put your life on hold: do what you have to do and the rest will follow. It really will, honestly!

Defining idea ...

'Success is getting what you want. Happiness is wanting what you get.'
DALE CARNEGIE

a way of spending time with your partner, friends, kids and the dog!

Strategy 2
Small changes over a long period of time will become an integral part of your lifestyle, unlike short-term tactics. Once you've lost your excess weight, the slimmer you will need fewer calories for maintenance.

Strategy 3
People who keep weight off combine aerobic activity with resistance training. This helps burn off calories and builds muscle, which uses up more calories than fat does.

Strategy 4
Research has found that if your weight loss is motivated by health reasons, it's more likely to stay off long term than if it's motivated by looks alone.

Strategy 5
Long-term weight losers have also developed a well-balanced approach to food and themselves in relation to it. They know they can get themselves back on track if they gain weight, by forgiving rather than blaming themselves.

This book is published by Infinite Ideas, creators of the acclaimed **52 Brilliant Ideas** series. If you found this book helpful, here are some other titles in the **Brilliant Little Ideas** series which you may also find interesting.

- **Be incredibly creative:** 52 brilliant little ideas to hone your mind
- **Be incredibly healthy:** 52 brilliant little ideas to look and feel fantastic
- **Catwalk looks:** 52 brilliant little ideas to look gorgeous always
- **Drop a dress size:** 52 brilliant little ideas to lose weight and stay slim
- **Enjoy great sleep:** 52 brilliant little ideas for bedtime bliss
- **Get fit:** 52 brilliant little ideas to win at the gym
- **Healthy children's lunches:** 52 brilliant little ideas for junk-free meals kids will love
- **Incredible sex:** 52 brilliant little ideas to take you all the way
- **Quit smoking for good:** 52 brilliant little ideas to kick the habit
- **Raising young children:** 52 brilliant little ideas for parenting under 5s
- **Relax:** 52 brilliant little ideas to chill out
- **Shape up your bum:** 52 brilliant little ideas for maximising your gluteus

For more detailed information on these books and others published by Infinite Ideas please visit www.infideas.com.

See reverse for order form.

Qty	Title	RRP
	Be incredibly creative	£5.99
	Be incredibly healthy	£4.99
	Catwalk looks	£5.99
	Drop a dress size	£5.99
	Enjoy great sleep	£5.99
	Get fit	£5.99
	Healthy children's lunches	£5.99
	Incredible sex	£5.99
	Quit smoking for good	£4.99
	Raising young children	£5.99
	Relax	£5.99
	Shape up your bum	£5.99
	Add £2.49 postage per delivery address	
	Total	

Name ....

Delivery address ....

....

....

E-mail.............................Tel (in case of problems) ....

By post Fill in all relevant details, cut out or copy this page and send along with a cheque made payable to Infinite Ideas. Send to: *Brilliant Little Ideas*, Infinite Ideas, 36 St Giles, Oxford OX1 3LD. **Credit card orders over the telephone** Call +44 (0) 1865 514 888. Lines are open 9am to 5pm Monday to Friday.

Please note that no payment will be processed until your order has been dispatched. Goods are dispatched through Royal Mail within 14 working days, when in stock. We never forward personal details on to third parties or bombard you with junk mail. The prices quoted are for UK and RoI residents only. If you are outside these areas please contact us for postage and packing rates. Any questions or comments please contact us on 01865 514 888 or email info@infideas.com.